OUT IN FRONT

GRACE AKALLO AND THE PURSUIT OF JUSTICE FOR CHILD SOLDIERS

MONROVIA, LIBERIA. 2003.

OUT IN FRONT

GRACE AKALLO AND THE PURSUIT OF JUSTICE FOR CHILD SOLDIERS

KEM KNAPP SAWYER

MORGAN REYNOLDS
PUBLISHING

GREENSBORO, NORTH CAROLINA

 To join the discussion about this title, please check out the Morgan Reynolds Readers Club on Facebook, or Like our company page to stay up to date on the latest Morgan Reynolds news!

OUT IN FRONT
GRACE AKALLO
AND THE PURSUIT OF JUSTICE FOR CHILD SOLDIERS

Copyright © 2015 by Morgan Reynolds Publishing

Library of Congress Cataloging-in-Publication Data
Sawyer, Kem Knapp.
Grace Akallo and the pursuit of justice for child soldiers / by Kem Knapp Sawyer. -- First edition.
       pages cm. -- (Out in front)
Includes bibliographical references and index.
ISBN 978-1-59935-456-9 -- ISBN 978-1-59935-457-6 (ebook)
1. Akallo, Grace--Juvenile literature. 2. Child soldiers--Uganda--Biography--Juvenile literature.
3. Child soldiers--Juvenile literature. 4. Child soldiers--Rehabilitation--Juvenile literature.
5. Girls--Crimes against--Juvenile literature. 6. Children and war--Juvenile literature. I. Title.
UB419.U33S28 2015 362.88092--dc23
[B]   2014041750

Printed in the United States of America
First Edition

Book cover and interior designed by:
Ed Morgan, navyblue design studio
Greensboro, NC

CONTENTS

A 2004 PHOTO OF STUDENTS AT ST. MARY'S COLLEGE IN ABOKE, UGANDA, WHERE 139 GIRLS WERE KIDNAPPED BY THE LORD'S RESISTANCE ARMY IN 1996.

CHAPTER ONE:
STOLEN IN THE NIGHT

In the early hours of October 9, 1996, fifteen-year-old Grace Akallo was fast asleep in a dormitory at a Catholic girls' boarding school in Uganda. Suddenly, she awakened to the sound of shattering windows and a blaze of flashlights. Her eyes popped open. Frantic school mates dashed around the room, screaming. Rocks hurled from outside the broken windows pelted the girls as they scattered. "I jumped under my bed and began crying out, 'Jesus, help me! Jesus, help me!'" Then the rattle of a new sound startled her: "BAM! BAM," followed by someone ramming the locked door to the dormitory. Next, a voice: "Open or we begin shooting!"

Outside of two locked dormitories were three hundred rebels of the Lord's Resistance Army (LRA), a militia led by Joseph Kony, an internationally sought-after former Catholic choir boy turned warlord who wants to topple the government in Uganda. Armed with loaded AK-47s, the rebels sent to St. Mary's that night were about the same age as the teenage girls they came to abduct. In fact, the girls recognized some of the boys, who had been kidnapped a month earlier from a nearby school.

The siege lasted four hours, until finally the insurgents threatened to throw a grenade into the room. One frightened girl tried to escape. "We were so terrified no one tried to stop the frantic girl who unbolted the door," Grace later recalled. "A rebel stormed in and slapped her face with the flat of a machete." Grace's night of terror did not end there. That night was the

AK-47

beginning of a seven-month ordeal that would forever change Grace's life. Little did she know that she, too, would become that which she feared—a child soldier.

The rebels dragged Grace and the other girls from beneath their beds. Outside of the dormitory, the rebels used shea butter to mark crosses on the girls' foreheads, shoulders, and chests. Next they "tied all 139 of us together so we couldn't escape," she later recalled. "Then, they marched us from the dorm into the darkness of night, machine guns stuck in our backs. We knew who they were. We'd long feared their arrival. Now we had to choose: Join the Lord's Resistance Army or die."

Throughout the world, children like Grace Akallo are forced into armed conflict. They serve as messengers, spies, cooks, porters, servants—and also as fighters. Some carry weapons and are sent to the front—others participate in guerrilla warfare. They might lead a raid, lie in ambush, or place landmines. Girls—who make up an estimated 10 to 30 percent of children abducted—are also especially vulnerable to sexual violence; they are subjected to rape and molestation, or are forced, like Grace Akallo, to become a sex slave (a "wife") to an older soldier.

Historically, children have been forced to fight in almost every region of the world; recently, child soldiers have been documented fighting in many countries, including Afghanistan, Iraq, Burma, Yemen, India, Chad, the Democratic Republic of Congo (DRC), Colombia, Philippines, Thailand, South Sudan, Somalia, Syria, and Grace Akallo's home country, Uganda. The number of children under eighteen involved in armed conflict in recent years is thought to be approximately 300,000, according to estimates by the United Nations Children's Fund (UNICEF). (Of that number, 120,000 are girls.)

Grace's story is both exceptional and tragically common.

CHAPTER TWO:
CHILDREN IN ARMED CONFLICT

SEPTEMBER 6, 1944 — THIS NAZI 'SUPERMAN'
APPEARS TO BE IN HIS 'TEENS' AND HIS
EXPRESSION IS NOT EXACTLY THAT OF
THE CONQUERING HERO AS AN AMERICAN
SOLDIER LOOKS AT THE LAD'S INJURY
WHILE AWAITING THE ARRIVAL OF A MEDIC.

Child soldiers are not a new phenomenon in world history. The presence of boys and girls on battlefields has been recorded and accepted in almost all cultures and societies. Knights of Medieval Europe used young boys as squires and pages. The most feared soldiers in ancient Greece came from the city-state of Sparta, where young boys began brutal military training at age seven. The Ottoman Turkish Empire drafted child soldiers from all over the empire to form the Sultan's Elite Corps, known as the Jannisary Corps.

Then there's the well-known, though unverified, tale of the 1212 "Children's Crusade," a march of thousands of unarmed boys from northern France and western Germany to the Holy Land to fight against the Saracen rulers of Jerusalem and to capture the Holy Sepulchre. One chronicler wrote, a year after the event, "Many thousands of boys, ranging in age from six years to full maturity, left the ploughs or carts that they were driving, the flocks that they were pasturing . . . despite the efforts of their parents, relatives and friends to make them draw back." Supposedly, only a few of the boys made it to the Holy Land. The majority died from hunger and disease, while others were captured and sold into slavery.

The reasons for children fighting have not changed significantly down through history. Many are forcibly recruited or kidnapped. Poverty and starvation drives others to join, while patriotism and vengeance motivates still others. And, in many instances, it is a matter of kill or be killed. During World War II, sixteen- and seventeen-year-old boys from Hitler's Youth Brigade manned an entire SS Panzer Tank Division, and ambushed and defeated Canadians trying to take Caen during the Normandy campaign. Toward the end of the war, the Germans even drafted boys as young as twelve into military service. And numbers of young Japanese boys volunteered to be Kamikaze suicide pilots, in a show of pride to their parents, friends, and emperor.

America's Boy Soldiers

During America's Civil War, tens of thousands of boys joined the Union and Confederate armies. Historians estimate that between 10 and 20 percent of Civil War soldiers were under eighteen, meaning 250,000 to 420,000 boys. Even a few teenage girls cut their hair to disguise themselves as men to sign up.

Union soldiers were supposed to be at least eighteen to enlist, but some boys lied about their age. Tall boys, or boys who were big for their age, joined unquestioned, as there was no way to check a birth date. The Confederacy did not have a minimum age limit, and many boys wanted to fight alongside their older brothers, fathers, uncles, and teachers.

As the Civil War dragged on and casualties on both sides mounted, desperate recruiters turned a blind eye when underage boys showed up to enlist. One fifteen-year-old Wisconsin boy, Elisha Stockwell Jr., later regretted his deception. "I want to say, as we lay there and the shells were flying over us, my thoughts went back to home, and I thought what a foolish boy I was to run away and get into such a mess as I was in. I would have been glad to have seen my father coming after me."

Most boys became drummers, fifers, buglers, messengers, orderlies, scouts, and stretcher bearers. In camp, they had all sorts of jobs, such as sorting mail, carrying water, rubbing down horses, gathering wood, and cooking for the soldiers. They also built roads, dug trenches, and served as "powder monkeys" on Civil War ships. Powder monkeys knotted and spliced ropes, sewed sails, and spotted oncoming ships atop of masts. Also, their small size made it easy for them to climb in and out of hatches and deliver gunpowder and ammunition to gunners.

On the battlefield anything could happen, and some boys ended up armed and forced into battle. John Cook, a fifteen-year-old Union bugle player, operated a cannon during the famous battle of Antietam. Orion Howe, a fourteen-year-old drummer, was severely wounded while retrieving ammunition during the battle of Vicksburg. Sixteen-year-old musician John A. Cockerill wrote about a boy soldier he came upon on the battlefield:

> I passed . . . the corpse of a beautiful boy in gray who lay with his blond curls scattered about his face and his hand folded peacefully across his breast. . . . He was about my age. . . . At the sight of the poor boy's corpse, I burst into a regular boo hoo and started on.

At least forty-eight boys under age eighteen, including eleven under sixteen, received the Congressional Medal of Honor for their valor during the Civil War.

SAMUEL W. DOBLE
CIVIL WAR

A NORTH VIETNAMESE GIRL POINTS A RIFLE AT A U.S. AIR FORCE LIEUTENANT, AS HE WALKS IN FRONT OF HER THROUGH VEGETATION DURING THE VIETNAM WAR. THE AMERICAN POW WAS COPILOT OF A PLANE BROUGHT DOWN IN NORTH VIETNAM BY NORTH VIETNAMESE FORCES IN 1967.

While child soldiers are not a new phenomenon, in recent decades the world has witnessed a new trend, the rise of children as warrior-killers. Though children did sometimes fight in the past, they most typically served in support roles, such as cooks, porters, and servants. But today's child soldiers are forced to the front line, expected to kill and commit atrocities, and made the subject of brutal punishments if they fail. One recent estimate suggests that children make up 80 percent of the fighting forces in more than thirty wars and armed conflicts worldwide.

In the Democratic Republic of the Congo, for example, where fighting has caused the death of more than 5 million people through combat, hunger, and disease, 30,000 children, enlisted by armed rebel groups as well as the state army, have taken part in raids and massacres. In Liberia, some 38,000 children took part in that country's wars from 1989 to 2003, where they were responsible for some of the most brutal and devastating combat.

Cambodia's Khmer Rouge was known to force young boys and girls to be executioners, often of their own parents and families. In Nepal, the revolutionary Maoist party recruited 4,500 soldiers under eighteen to fight in that country's civil war (1996-2006). In efforts to overthrow the monarchy the Maoists instituted a "one-family, one-child" recruitment policy. One seventeen-year-old girl recalled, "They took me by force. The two ladies who came to our house were trying to convince me, but I kept refusing. They said they would kill me, but I still refused . . . and then they threatened they would make cuts on my body and pour chili pepper in the cuts. Then I was too scared and had to go with them."

During Sri Lanka's civil war (1983-2009), the militant rebel group the Tamil Tigers routinely recruited children ages eleven to sixteen for the "Baby Brigade." In preparation the youth spent four months in the jungle—they watched combat videos and learned to use weapons and explosives. The first child to show a sign of homesickness was beaten in front of the other children. Both boys and girls were trained for suicide bombing and given deadly cyanide pills to take if they were captured. The Tamil Tigers even had special denim jackets made to fit children and hide suicide explosives.

The Palestinian group Hamas, and the extremist terrorists of the Taliban have also used young boys as suicide bombers. Elsewhere in the Middle East, during the civil war in Syria that began in 2011, the Islamic State of Iraq and Syria (ISIS) recruited youth for combat positions by offering free schooling and weapon training. "At first I was so scared . . . then I got used to it," said Ayman, who started fighting for the Free Syrian Army brigade in the Syrian town of Salqin at the age of fifteen.

A PALESTINIAN BOY CLIMBS UNDER BARBED WIRE DURING A GRADUATION CEREMONY OF A MILITARY-STYLE SUMMER CAMP ORGANIZED BY THE HAMAS MOVEMENT

Children who are poor, hungry, or homeless are most likely to be abducted or recruited as soldiers. The military or armed groups provide them with clothing, food, and shelter. "I heard that the rebels at least were eating so I joined them," explained one boy from the Congo. In return for food and shelter, the children obey orders. They are not prone to fear, and often take risks adults would not. Their leaders may give them alcohol or drugs to ease their inhibitions. Sometimes the child soldiers' loyalty is tested: They are asked to kill family or friends as a test of loyalty to the leader. Those who fail the test are often killed themselves.

While many abducted children seek to escape from captors and their life of forced combat, others become indoctrinated in the violent lifestyle of the soldier. Trained to commit violent acts, and used to being rewarded for doing so, these children develop highly aggressive behaviors that they often inflict on other child soldiers. Furthermore, these aggressive personalities, developed out of fear and desperation for survival, make it harder for these children to rejoin their friends and families after they stop fighting (if they survive).

"I returned to my home village with my AK, the first time since I joined [Liberia's notorious guerrilla leader Charles Taylor]," a former child soldier now in his thirties recalled. "I was 11, 12 maybe. My mother asked if she could hug me. I said no. She asked if she could shake my hand. I said she should just get me a glass of water. That attachment, mother to son, was completely broken. The revolution did that."

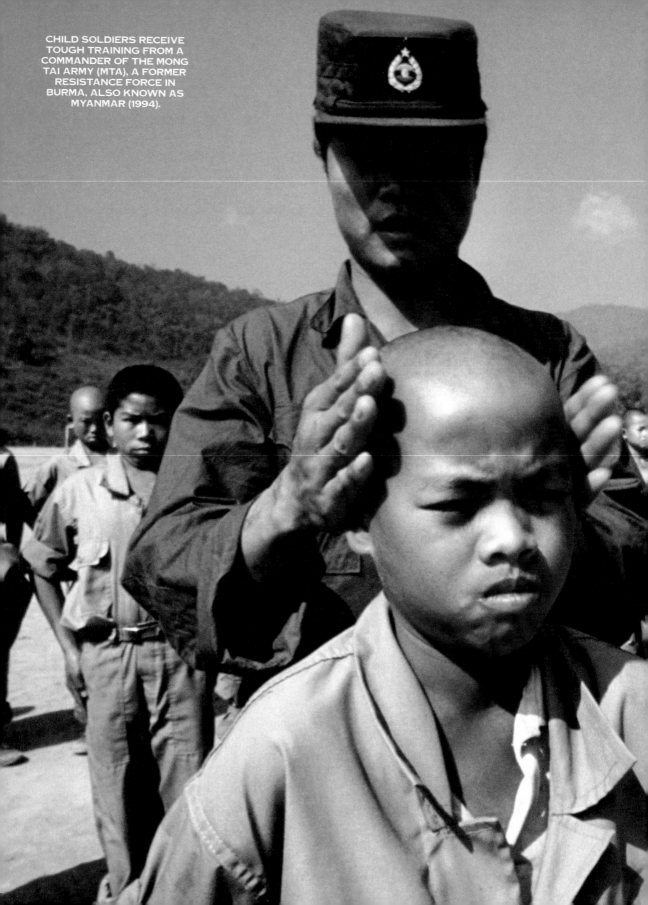

CHILD SOLDIERS RECEIVE TOUGH TRAINING FROM A COMMANDER OF THE MONG TAI ARMY (MTA), A FORMER RESISTANCE FORCE IN BURMA, ALSO KNOWN AS MYANMAR (1994).

For some children, the military unit takes the place of family they may have lost. Young soldiers bond with others in their group and see their leader as a father figure. In Sierra Leone's ten-year civil war, from 1991 to 2001, 80 percent of the fighters in the rebel Revolutionary United Front were between seven and fourteen, and they called their leader "Pappy." This familial feeling is another way that armed groups are able to manipulate children and ensure their absolute loyalty.

The National People's Army in the Philippines has recruited children to fight in a conflict that began in 1969. One girl explained that her father had a big stick that he used to beat her and her brother. However, once she joined the rebel movement, "it's like I have a mother, a father and elder siblings but we get along well with each other even if we don't even know where each of us comes from."

Militaries and other armed groups allow young soldiers little control over their lives. Most child soldiers are between the ages of fourteen and eighteen, yet many are as young as nine. Sometimes they sound tough, even ruthless. But they are still vulnerable. "I'm not afraid to die, but I'm afraid to die so young," a child soldier from Colombia, who learned to use a gun at the age of eight, said. "You can't think about the future here, because the future is a coffin."

CHAPTER THREE:
THE DEN OF DEATH

An aerial view over northern Uganda. Thick jungle forests in Uganda, southern Sudan, and the Congo have provided cover for Kony and his notorious LRA for almost three decades. A *New York Times* article described Kony's "turf" as "a vast expanse the size of California in the middle of Africa. . . . Picture towering trees that blot out the sun, endless miles of elephant grass, and swirling brown rivers that coil like intestines and are infested with crocodiles," one of which "ate a Ugandan" taking part in the hunt for Kony. Despite an international drive to close the net on the rebel leader and bring him to trial at the International Criminal Court for war crimes and crimes against humanity, the warlord continues to evade capture and cut a wide and bloody swath across several central African nations.

Grace Akallo had always loved school. Starting at age six, she walked ten miles to school every morning, carrying the lunch that her grandfather had prepared. The school, attended by three hundred students, was in a grass hut with a thatched roof that often leaked. Grace didn't care.

She was born in 1981 into a family of three sisters and one brother in Kaberikole, a small village in northern Uganda. She lived with her mother and maternal grandparents. Her father left the village a few years after Grace's birth, under pressure from the grandparents to follow tradition and pay a dowry as proof of marriage to Grace's mother and for the sake of their daughter. But with no money to pay, the father moved to the nearby town of Lira and married another woman.

In Kaberikole, Grace's mother did most of the farming. She plowed the fields and tended to the crops: sorghum, cassava, corn, beans, and sweet potatoes, which were sold and traded in the market. Without an education, Grace knew that farming would eventually be her fate. Fortunately, a kind uncle offered to pay her fees to attend primary, or elementary, school. But just as she was about to begin junior high school, the uncle was killed in a car accident, and all hope of Grace continuing her education died with him. Devastated, she dropped out of school and began helping her mother.

There was one bright light in her life. Grace liked listening to her grandfather tell stories. Her favorite was when her grandfather told stories about his own father, a strong and respected man, and how Grace might someday be like him. "When he said that maybe I was going to be like his father, I would crawl toward him and give him a hug because I loved listening to the heroic stories. I especially liked it when my grandpa said I would be the next hero," she recalled.

Grace missed a year of school, but then her father returned with news that he had secured a spot for her at St. Mary's. At age fourteen, Grace passed a national exam qualifying her to attend high school, and soon enrolled at the prestigious St. Mary's, located outside Aboke, in northern Uganda. Attending the school would be the first step toward getting a college education. Grace said, "I was determined to be the first person to go to university in my village."

Grace liked St. Mary's, considered one of the best schools in Uganda. The school was run by an Italian nun, Sister Alba. She was assisted by Sister Rachele, who also taught biology. They kept the girls to a tight schedule, starting every day at six in the morning, followed by chores, classes, meals, study periods, and then a little time for reading or socialization. They were so protective of their charges, and the school so isolated, that the students of St. Mary's often saw no outsiders until the end of the term.

But on October 9, 1996, some outsiders came to St. Mary's. It was Uganda's Independence Day, and the whole school celebrated. The students sang and danced, but that evening Sister Alba told the girls that they would not be allowed to watch a movie as was the custom on a holiday. They must read quietly in their rooms. Word had spread of the pending approach of the Lord's Resistance Army (LRA).

Sister Rachele had spent the day trying to find government soldiers to guard the dormitories that night, and she had even received a promise of protection. However, by midnight, no soldiers had arrived. At 2:15 a.m., the school's night watchman knocked on the window of Sister Rachele's convent room. "The rebels are here," he said. Sister Rachele made a decision she would later regret: To prevent the rebels from forcing her to unlock the dorm doors, she hid in tall grass behind the school.

MEMBERS OF THE LORD'S RESISTANCE ARMY (2006)

The LRA was a particularly notorious rebel group, begun in 1987 to oppose Ugandan president Yoweri Museveni. Museveni had come to power himself heading up a rebel group called the National Resistance Army (NRA), which became the Ugandan People's Defence Force (UPDF) when Museveni officially took power. The roots of the conflict went back even further, though, to when British colonial rule of the territory that would become Uganda exacerbated conflicts between various ethnic groups, including the Acholi people, who comprised most of the LRA leadership. In their struggle for power, Museveni and the NRA had committed many atrocities: looting and burning villages, raping women, and massacring people, many of whom were Acholi. This savagery caused the members of the LRA to resort to similarly heinous violence in their own campaigns.

Winston Churchill and King Daudi Cwa II of Buganda in Kampala, Uganda, in 1907. From 1894 to 1962 Uganda was a protectorate of the British Empire. Before colonization, the area was a collection of different ethnic and religious groups, among which there had always been tensions. The British exacerbated those tensions by signing a treaty with the Bugandans, the biggest ethnic group in southern Uganda, in 1890, followed by a declaration of a British protectorate over Uganda in 1894. British favor and protection of the Bugandans upset northern tribes, over which the British allowed the Bugandans to rule. This system of ethnic patronage continues to haunt current politics. Ugandan president Museveni's victory in 1986, at the head of an army primarily comprised of fighters from the west and central regions, sparked opposition in northern Acholiland, where Joseph Kony was born in 1961.

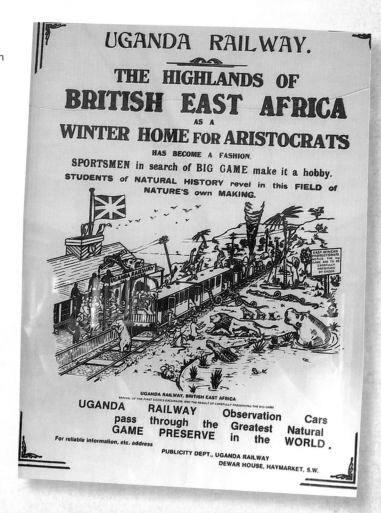

An ad for the Uganda Railway, known colloquially as the Lunatic Express and the Iron Snake. Built by the British government between 1896 and 1901 to expand its domination in Africa, the mostly single-lane railway links the interior of Uganda to the Kenyan coast at Mombassa.

There was a religious element to the LRA's campaign as well. Its leader, Joseph Kony, an Acholi, claimed that all of his actions were the will of God. He used his status as a religious leader to further influence and control his followers, who called him father or Lakwena, the Acholi word for one who serves the holy spirit. He claimed that all of the violence perpetrated by the LRA was justified by the Bible, yet his prayers, chants, and rants were a mix of Christian, Muslim, and tribal spiritual beliefs, as well as superstition.

The LRA was known to abduct children and force them to fight. Doing this not only bolstered the LRA's numbers, but complicated the government's own defensive strategies. The government couldn't attack LRA forces without killing many of these abducted children; in effect, killing civilians and angering the country's population. The LRA had attacked St. Mary's school looking for young people to abduct and force into their army. Grace Akallo was one of the more than 30,000 children abducted by the Lord's Resistance Army between 1988 and 2004.

Marching into the night with the LRA soldiers, Grace was tired and cold. In the chaos of being forced out of the dorms, she had been unable to put on shoes or any clothes over her nightgown. One of her classmates had grabbed some clothes as they were leaving the school, and she handed Grace a green dress and sweatshirt. The more Grace walked—miles and miles of walking—the more her feet ached. "Sharp stones and thorns dug into my shoeless feet. During a short rest, I tied banana leaves to my feet as makeshift shoes." The rope tying the girls together cut into her wrist, leaving it raw. She stumbled but still kept walking.

As the hours passed, the girls were forced to keep moving. The soldiers gave them no food or water, and they grew hungrier as the night passed.

After the sun rose, they heard familiar voices. Sister Rachele and John Bosco, a geography teacher from St. Mary's, had come after them. The LRA soldiers had raided candy and soda from the school, and Sister Rachele and Bosco had been able to follow the trail of discarded wrappers and bottles. Mariano Ocaya Lagira, the LRA commander, ordered the rebels to halt and pointed his gun at John Bosco. Sister Rachele grabbed

SISTER RACHELE

Lagira by the arm. "I must take the girls back," she said. "They're so young. They must return with me."

Lagira refused to listen and told Sister Rachele to return to the convent. Sister Rachele thought the LRA soldiers would respect her as a nun, but they threatened to kill and rape her. Lagira ignored her pleas for the girls' release and forced them to continue marching.

Still Sister Rachele and John Bosco followed close behind them. They walked all morning and all afternoon. That evening, when they arrived at a village, Sister Rachele fell to her knees and again pleaded with the commander. "I'm not a god. Get up," Lagira told her. "Of the one hundred and thirty-nine girls you may take back one hundred and nine. I will keep thirty." He had already selected the thirty that would stay in the LRA's custody. Grace was one of them.

Sister Rachele objected, but Lagira told her if she wouldn't accept that offer, he would keep all 139 of the captive girls. She realized that she had no choice but to take back the 109 girls Lagira would release, and try to rescue the rest later. And to instill fear and discipline in the remaining captives, Lagira told them, "If one of you escapes, the rest will be killed."

After two weeks of walking, Grace and the other Aboke captives reached Kony's military training camp in southern Sudan. There, the soldiers gave each of the girls a cheap AK-47 and taught them to dismantle the guns, clean them, and reassemble them. "The first thing, you're beaten," Grace would testify later. "The beating is to initiate you into the army. The second thing, you're forced to kill someone."

The soil in Sudan was barren and sandy, and there were no houses or roads in sight. Grace dug holes in the earth to find drinking water and scavenged for rats, roots, leaves, and wild fruits. "Hunger will teach you how to shoot," one of the rebels told Grace. The choice was clear: Grace could fight or she could stay in the camp, to die of starvation or be killed by the rebels. "It was survival of the fittest," Grace said. "You had to shoot that gun to get food, you had to fight at the frontline to survive."

Before battle, LRA soldiers spread oil from the nuts of trees on their bodies. Sometimes they used the oil to draw a cross on themselves. Joseph Kony, their leader, had convinced them that the oil had special powers to protect them—that bullets would bounce off their skin if it were coated with this oil. It didn't work; some of the Aboke girls and other abducted children were killed in combat. Kony also used psychological techniques to control the children, telling them that he knew their thoughts and could tell when they were considering escaping. "I tried to stop thinking," Grace said. "And it's not a joke—they bring people and they kill them in front of you and they say they were thinking of escape."

KONY, AS SEEN IN AN IMAGE TAKEN FROM REUTERS TV IN NAIROBI, KENYA, MAY 24, 2006. FILMED IN AN UNKNOWN LOCATION IN SOUTHERN SUDAN, IT IS ONE OF ONLY A FEW IMAGES OF KONY SEEN IN YEARS.

Like most young women abducted by the LRA, Grace was forced to become "a wife." She became the fifth wife of a trusted Kony lieutenant. Her "husband" had "bloodshot eyes" and was "old enough to be my grandfather," she said. The term "wife" was misleading: Grace was actually being forced to be a concubine, or sex slave. "I was an innocent young girl. I had never known a man in my life until that day," Grace said.

Grace and her "husband" traveled from village to village with the other soldiers—setting fire to houses, shooting, and taking with them everything that they could carry. Even children as young as seven joined in the looting. Unless they were pregnant, girls were expected to fight alongside boys. "What makes a girl child soldier different is the sexual abuse that they are forced to endure," Akallo later recalled. "Most girls were sexually abused, including me. I was lucky I did not return home with a child, or get infected with HIV or any other disease. Many of these girls had to give birth while in captivity, some of them had to go fighting with children on their backs, and some gave birth on the battlefield," she said.

All the child soldiers dutifully followed orders, including the order to kill. "At first, I was scared of even beating someone else because I was afraid they would get hurt," said Grace. "When I was forced to kill another human being . . . that really altered me. It affected me psychologically. Seeing somebody suffer because they are being mutilated is the worst thing you can ever witness."

In an instant, Grace's relatively easy life in a quiet village had turned into a grisly nightmare, or as she would later put it, "a den of death." Back home in Kaberikole, she used to walk three miles to attend St. Augustine Anglican Church to sing in the choir on Sundays and to help the needy. Her surname, Akallo, means "jumping over problems" in her language, but after her indoctrination into the LRA, Grace felt she had become a non-person. She did not allow herself time to think or feel or pray. "When I did pray, I no longer prayed to escape. I wanted to die. I prayed, 'If my time must come. Lord, please take me. . . . But let me see my parents, just once, before I die.'"

CHAPTER FOUR:

"GET UP AND GO"

For seven months, Grace Akallo remained in the custody of the Lord's Resistance Army. She wanted to kill herself—and made three attempts. "Every time I tried to pull the trigger of the gun, God brought someone to grab the gun away from me," she said later.

Grace dreamed that she would escape. The dream gave her the courage to look for an opportunity. One day, the Ugandan army attacked the LRA base camp. The fighting lasted for several days, and hundreds of child soldiers were cut down by mortar fire.

Grace saw that no one was watching her. And she heard a voice speaking to her, saying, "Get up and go." She began walking and did not look back. Only seven months had passed since she had been abducted, but it felt like seven years.

After three days of trudging through the bush, Grace met a group of eight girls who like her had escaped from the LRA. The girls joined Grace, and they traveled south toward the Ugandan border. Several days later they came across men from the Dinka ethnic group. They were not LRA soldiers, but members of the Sudan People's Liberation Army (SPLA), a militant group who were allies of the Ugandan army and enemies of the LRA. Initially, the Dinka were suspicious of the girls, who did not speak their language. Eventually, however, the men recognized that the emaciated girls needed help. Together they trekked into the night single file, their path lit by stars. When they all arrived at the army barracks of the SPLA, they showed the girls a room where they could sleep.

SUDAN PEOPLE'S LIBERATION ARMY (SPLA) TROOPS ON PATROL OUTSIDE THE MILITARY STRONGHOLD OF THE SPLA IN SOUTHERN SUDAN. THE SPLA ARE MOSTLY DINKA, AND ARE THE REBEL RESISTANCE GROUP THAT HELPED PROTECT THE DINKA PEOPLE DURING THE WAR.

John Garang, the SPLA commander, came to speak with Grace. He was from the Dinka and had studied economics in the United States. She told him that she was an Aboke girl who had been abducted from school. Garang listened to her story and then put the girls under the protection of Ugandan soldiers—his allies. That day they were taken by car to an army camp in northern Uganda.

A Ugandan army commander and his wife took special care of Grace and brought her to a hospital for treatment. After leaving the hospital, Grace returned to their house. Sister Rachele came to see Grace as soon as she heard that she had escaped. Ever since the abduction, Sister Rachele had tried everything to save the thirty Aboke girls who had remained captive. She had talked to the president of Uganda as well as the president of Sudan, visited with ambassadors, and sent a message to Pope John Paul II. Together with parents of the kidnapped Aboke girls, she had founded the Concerned Parents Association, a lobbying group that launched a successful international campaign to get the countries that gave aid to Uganda, including the United States, to put pressure on the Museveni government to end the war.

Once Grace regained her strength, she visited her family in Kaberikole and spent a month with them. But readjusting to her life was difficult. "I used to isolate myself a lot . . . not because I suffered—I was beaten, I was sexually assaulted—but mostly because I had left my friends behind. I felt guilty of surviving. I felt guilty of being free when my friends were still with the rebels," Grace said.

The ex-child soldier did not talk to her family or friends about her life with the rebels. There was so much she did not want to share.

Eventually, she returned to St. Mary's. However, she stayed "for only a short time before the rebels again neared Aboke." Not wanting a repeat of the horror she had faced as a LRA soldier, Grace fled to her father's home, in Lira, where she enrolled in a new school, St. Catherine's. "There, I tried in vain to keep my past secret. Everyone in Uganda knows the LRA forces kids to join their uprising. But still, people wrongly think you must like killing and stealing. My classmates taunted me by calling me 'Kony's wife!'"

After she graduated from high school, Grace wanted to fulfill her dream of attending college. But, she said, "My parents told me I should not study." They advised her to get married and raise children. Grace felt compelled to follow her dream, however, and enrolled in the Uganda Christian University. She also started to work as a volunteer at the Rachele Rehabilitation Centre, a shelter for former child soldiers who needed medical care, food, and counseling. It was founded by the Belgian journalist Els De Temmerman and named for Sister Rachele.

Later, Grace transferred to Gordon College, a small school north of Boston, Massachusetts. She graduated at age twenty-six with a degree in communications, and also studied international relations. Grace went on to receive her master's degree in international development and social change at Clark University in Worcester, Massachusetts.

Her time as a child soldier was far behind her. She was safe. As much as she had been through, Grace knew she was lucky to have survived and emerged into a normal life. But her story was exceptional; many others were not so lucky.

Where is Joseph Kony?

The whereabouts of Joseph Kony are unknown. Chased out of Uganda in 2005, he is thought to be in the borderlands of South Sudan, the Democratic Republic of the Congo, and Central African Republic. In 2005, the International Criminal Court in The Hague, in the Netherlands, issued arrest warrants for Kony and three of his top commanders, and regional armies continue to hunt for Kony with the help of U.S. soldiers. To date, however, he has eluded capture and continues to abduct children. According to a recent United Nations report, during the reporting period of July 2009 to February 2012, nearly six hundred children were abducted and recruited by the LRA, mostly in the Democratic Republic of the Congo, but also in Central African Republic and South Sudan. One of the few outsiders who has attempted to negotiate peace with Kony is Betty Bigombe, a Ugandan minister. In 2005, Bigombe risked her life to meet face-to-face with Kony, who prophesied about his death: "I know exactly how I am going to die. I am going to die like Hitler. One day people will wake up and find that I have been dead for some time."

Grace, like so many, wanted Kony to face the consequences for his crimes, but she knew that capturing him was only one step towards facing the problems of child soldiers. "I want Joseph Kony to be captured, I want him to disappear," she said. "But at the same time, if all the resources are directed towards him, then what about the people who suffered under him—what kind of justice are they getting? . . . Even if we capture Kony today . . . is that the end of everything? After tomorrow, what is the next step?"

Indeed, many other groups and militias throughout the world have taken to utilizing tactics similar to Kony's, capturing children and forcing them onto the front lines. In 2014, for example, the Nigeria-based terrorist group Boko Haram (who came to international notoriety when they kidnapped more than two hundred school girls from the village of Chibok, Borno) was known to abduct boys and force them to fight with the terrorists, or face death. As long as there is war, it seems, there will be those who seek to exploit and victimize children for their own advantage.

GRACE AKALLO AT A NEWS CONFERENCE
WITH U.S. REPRESENTATIVE CHRIS
SMITH OF NEW JERSEY IN APRIL 2006.
SMITH ANNOUNCED LEGISLATION THAT
ADDRESSES THE PRACTICE OF ABDUCTION.

CHAPTER FIVE:
ADVOCATE FOR JUSTICE AND PEACE

When she was thirteen years old, Mary Goll joined a militia in her homecountry of Liberia. The nation was in the midst of its second civil war, and Mary initially fought on the side of then president Charles Taylor (who had seized power just a few years earlier). Born into poverty in the midst of Liberia's first civil war, Mary grew up in an environment of abuse and violence. The military offered stability and a way for Mary to take care of herself, so she let herself be recruited. She rose through the ranks, eventually becoming a commander. Mary spent the next three years fighting in Liberia's civil war, a conflict marked by extreme violence and atrocity. Both sides made extensive use of child soldiers, and the violence perpetrated by and against child combatants attracted international attention and revulsion.

When the war ended, Mary voluntarily surrendered. But she'd spent her formative teenage years as a fighter. Returning to civilian life, Mary had no skills or prospects for a job. She became addicted to drugs and soon turned to prostitution to support herself. With the help of a social worker, she eventually quit drugs and opened a bar in a poor neighborhood, from which she was able to earn a good living. But even years later, Mary was still prone to violence, attacking men who spoke to her disrespectfully and abusing the young girl who helped manage her bar. Her days as a soldier were over, but Mary continued to fight.

For many child soldiers like Mary, the struggle doesn't end when the fighting stops. Throughout the world, child soldiers who survive the battle and return home are faced with a new set of challenges as they attempt to restart the lives that had been brought to a halt. Returning to their hometowns and villages, they are not greeted warmly. Instead many are shunned by their family and community, and feel a deep sense of shame. Villagers who lost loved ones or saw their homes and schools destroyed often associate these returning youth with the fighting and the looting. Furthermore, they fear the return of ex-combatants as a threat to future stability.

Many of the children returning from years in war have physical scars and wounds from their time on the frontlines. Some militias amputate limbs as a form of punishment. While in the conflict in Liberia, young soldiers who showed too much emotion at the atrocities they were asked to commit were permanently blinded. Wounds from bullets, land-mine explosions, or mutilations torment many former child soldiers, causing chronic pain and serving as reminders of their terrible ordeals.

MEMBERS OF THE SINGLE LEG AMPUTEE SPORTS CLUB OF SIERRA LEONE PLAYING FOOTBALL IN FREETOWN, SIERRA LEONE, IN 2006. THE MEMBERS ARE FORMER CHILD SOLDIERS.

More than just physical wounds, many former child soldiers have severe psychological scars. Research has shown that many children forced to fight in wars end up with severe and debilitating psychological problems afterwards. One study found that between 27 and 35 percent of former Ugandan child soldiers suffered from Post-Traumatic Stress Disorder (PTSD). (Symptoms of the disease include depression, debilitating flashbacks, extreme paranoia, guilt, and other things that make living a normal life incredibly difficult). Other studies have shown large numbers of former child soldiers are prone to depression and suicidal thoughts, and a study in Sri Lanka found higher rates of PTSD in children conscripted to fight than in adults.

Many others suffer from drug and substance abuse problems. Some became addicted during their times as soldiers, when military leaders encouraged drug use amongst child soldiers to numb their fear and emotions, and make them more compliant and easily manipulated. Others become addicted upon returning from war, when they use drugs to drown out their pain or deal with PTSD. The result is many former child soldiers suffer from drug related health problems, and many die of overdose.

Child soldiers who were sexually abused face another set of challenges when reintegrating into civilian life. Often, they have been given sexually transmitted diseases by their abusers. In Uganda, for example, HIV/AIDS is a major problem. A Ugandan health organization has estimated that in addition to HIV/AIDS, many of the sexually abused child soldiers also suffer from syphilis.

Girl child soldiers face their own unique difficulties. Many of the home countries of former child soldiers have highly conservative and traditional cultures that emphasize female chastity and virtue. Even though many of the girls were forced into sex slavery, they are still viewed as shamed or impure upon returning home, and are ostracized by their communities. They have trouble finding jobs or mates, and are often even shunned by their own families.

"Some of them are so destitute and disempowered that they don't believe they are human beings anymore," says a researcher studying female child soldiers. Many also were impregnated by their rapists and find themselves unable to love a child they did not want and whose presence is a constant reminder of the crime committed against them. Also, the majority of these girls are unable to provide for their children. This leads to more poverty, which in turn creates environments in which militias are able to recruit poor young people to fight, creating a dangerous cycle of violence.

A FORMER LORD'S RESISTANCE ARMY CHILD SOLDIER IS
DOING BEAD WORK TO SUPPLEMENT HER INCOME WHILE HER
CHILD SLEEPS ON HER BACK NEAR GULU, IN UGANDA.

In an attempt to break the cycle, governments from around the world have established standards of international law and protocols that ban the use of child soldiers and protect the rights of children. In 1989, the United Nations (UN) Convention on the Rights of the Child and subsequent protocols limited the use of children in military forces.

In 1996, the secretary-general of the UN asked Mozambican humanitarian Graça Machel to study the impact of armed conflict on children. The report by Machel, who is the widow of both Nelson Mandela of South Africa and Mozambican president Samora Machel, drew attention to the needs of children in combat situations, influencing policy for years to come. Various measures were put in place to protect children in combat situations. In 2007, for example, then President George W. Bush signed into law the Child Soldiers Accountability Act, making it a crime to recruit soldiers under the age of fifteen, anyplace in the world. Other countries adopted similar laws.

The UN continues to seek ways to enforce the protocols. In 2012, Leila Zerrougui was appointed "the UN special representative of the secretary general for Children and Armed Conflict" and she has become a strong advocate for the "Children, Not Soldiers" movement.

But government organizations can only do so much, especially in areas where armed militants have no interest in (or even knowledge of) government regulations. To pick up the slack and help out in ways that the government cannot, many small, grassroots non-government organizations have formed to help child soldiers and protect children in the future.

A YOUNG WOMAN ATTENDS A SPECIAL CEREMONY WITH HUNDREDS OF SYMBOLIC RED HANDS ON THE LAWN OF THE UNITED NATIONS EUROPEAN HEADQUARTERS IN GENEVA, SWITZERLAND, FEBRUARY 12, 2002. MORE THAN 300,000 CHILDREN, MOSTLY BETWEEN FIFTEEN AND SEVENTEEN BUT SOME AS YOUNG AS NINE, ARE THOUGHT TO BE WAGING WAR IN SOME FORTY DIFFERENT CONFLICTS AROUND THE WORLD, RANGING FROM THE GUERRILLA STRUGGLES OF COLOMBIA TO AFRICA'S OFTEN GRUESOME CIVIL WARS.

One such organization is the Children's Movement for Peace, founded in Colombia in 1996. Since 1964, some 11,000 children have fought in Colombia's decades-long civil war, fighting for both the government and opposition forces. Boys, as young as nine, planted bombs at polling stations and military checkpoints. Other child soldiers served as spies, made and deployed mines, and guarded victims of kidnapping.

The Children's Movement for Peace was started by children from across Colombia with the goal of helping to end the conflict and "demobilize" (release from military service) child soldiers. As many as 100,000 young people became involved in the movement's peace-making activities and clean-up campaigns. They planted trees and started play groups for children affected by violence. Furthermore, they worked to reunite former child soldiers with their families and their communities.

47

"Children are the seeds of peace; we are the seeds that will stop the war," a young leader in the Children's Movement said.

Another important organization, the *Bureau pour le Volontariat au Service de l'Enfance et de la Santé* (Voluntary Office at the Service of Childhood and Health) or BVES in Bukavu, a city in eastern Congo, sponsors thirty-five transitional centers for children affected by armed combat. The staff, some of whom are former child soldiers, counsel ex-combatants, often reassuring the youth that they will not be recaptured. They encourage them to return to school, assist in job training, and help trace family members.

In the Congolese city of Goma, a number of different organizations show the variety of ways people attempt to help children returning from war. At the Don Bosco Center Ngangi, former child soldiers (and other young people) can study welding, cooking and pastry, sewing, hairdressing, farming, and woodworking. Young mothers can find support for their small children. They take comfort in being together—their classmates become family. At Amani, an orphanage and rehabilitation center in the hills outside Goma, in the Congo, small children are nurtured, while ex-child soldiers receive job training in sewing and tailoring. When they leave, they are provided with their own sewing machine so they can set up their own businesses. The Promote Youth Basketball program (the PJB Academy) provides more than skill training for its participants, including former child soldiers. They learn discipline, etc the value of hard work, and team spirit. Busara, a dance company, provides intensive dance therapy workshops

STELA ANGOM, SIXTEEN, AND LUCY ADONG, EIGHTEEN, LEARN HOW TO USE A SEWING MACHINE AT THE GUSCO (GULU SUPPORT THE CHILDREN ORGANIZATION) CHILD SOLDIER REHABILITAION CENTER IN GULU, UGANDA. THE CHILDREN ARE TRAINED IN LIFE SKILLS AT THE CAMP SO THEY WILL BE ABLE TO SUPPORT THEMSELVES. THE CENTER HAS REHABILITATED MORE THAN 2,300 CHILDREN SINCE ITS FOUNDING IN 1994.

for former child soldiers. Congolese co-directors Chiku and Chito Lwambo use movement and improvisation to increase the former soldiers' self-confidence and help them smile and laugh, some for the first time since leaving the army.

For many former child soldiers, programs such as these do not just provide education and camaraderie. These are the only outlets that allow them to connect to others and to feel whole once again.

UNICEF AMBASSADOR ISHMAEL BEAH

For many former child soldiers, the key to moving on and reclaiming the part of themselves lost by being forced into combat is sharing their story and talking with other people who understand. In 2007, Ismael Beah wrote and published his story in *A Long Way Gone: Memoirs of a Boy Soldier*. Recruited at age thirteen, Beah fought for Sierra Leone's national army, looting, killing rebels, and raiding villages. At age sixteen, he was rescued by UNICEF, and later moved to the United States. "If you are alive, there is hope for a better day and something good to happen," Beah wrote. "If there is nothing good left in the destiny of a person, he or she will die."

When Grace Akallo returned to her family after escaping the LRA, she spent many long hours with the young people at the Rachele Rehabilitation Centre. "I loved helping kids learn to forgive those who so horribly abused them," said Grace. "It helped me as much as it did them." She also understood that letting the children talk about their pain was helpful. "If a kid doesn't cry, it's hard for him to open up. Deep inside he's still in pain." As for her own tears, Grace said,

> maybe someday, when there is peace, I will sit down and cry for myself. But right now, I think what is happening needs to be stopped. I have to use the life that I was given for a purpose. . . . not to mourn over what happened to me. I was supported—I went to school, and I have a family that supports me and loves me. But what about the girls who are still suffering? They are still being beaten. They are still rejected. They still don't have homes or family support or access to any resources or education or health care. Nothing!

After coming to America and finishing her studies, Grace realized she could greatly help her fellow child soldiers by sharing her story with the world. She wrote an autobiography titled *Girl Soldier: A Story of Hope for Northern Uganda's Children*, co-authored with Faith McDonnell. Her book received much attention and acclaim, and Grace has become an advocate against the use of children in armed conflict—testifying on Capitol Hill and at the United Nations, speaking out on college campuses, schools, and churches. At a Congressional hearing, she told U.S. senators, "I have told my own story but the stories you have not heard are thousands-fold. There are dozens of armies and rebel groups who continue to ruin the lives of children in the same ways around the world. I'm here to remind you of the very real suffering of these children who are hoping for you to act."

Now living permanently in the United States, Grace has started her own non-profit, non-governmental organization called United Africans for Women and Children Rights. The group advocates for the rights of former child soldiers, working to ensure that they are not prosecuted for any actions they were forced to commit, and that they have access to medical care, trauma counseling, and education. The group also works to ensure the rights of women to pursue education and careers, and helps to spread important information about sexual health, family planning, and HIV prevention.

Nearly twenty years have passed since her kidnapping, yet it may take a lifetime for Grace, now married with two children she calls "a gift," to fully process the emotional trauma of her past. "I may never know why God allowed what happened." Grace said. "But without God's protection, I would be dead now."

Of the thirty St. Mary's girls abducted in 1996, five are dead and many returned home with babies, HIV/AIDS, or both. The last of the Aboke girls returned home in 2009, with a twenty-one-month-old baby, whom she said Kony fathered.

"I believe God spared me for a reason," Grace said. "There's work He has for me. I'm daily asking God to use my dark past to help my suffering people. I understand what these child soldiers have been through. That makes it easier for me to help them."

SOURCES

CHAPTER 1: STOLEN IN THE NIGHT

p. 8,   "I jumped under my bed . . ." Grace Akallo, "I Survived Hell," as told to Deann Alford, *Ignite Your Faith* 65, no. 8 (March 2007), www.christianitytoday.com/iyf/truelifestories/ithappenedtome/7.38.html.

p. 8,   "we were so terrified . . ." Ibid.

p. 9,   "tied all 139 . . . die," Ibid.

CHAPTER 2: CHILDREN IN ARMED CONFLICT

p. 12,   "Many thousands of boys . . ." "The Children's Crusade: Fairly Holy Innocents," *The Economist*, December 21, 2000.

p. 13,   "I want to say . . ." Cate Lineberry, "The Boys of War," *New York Times*, October 4, 2011.

p. 13,   "I passed . . ." Ibid.

p. 15,   "They took me . . ." Human Rights Watch. *Children in the Ranks: The Maoists' Use of Child Soldiers in Nepal.* February 2, 2007, p. 6. http://www.hrw.org/node/11040/section/6

p. 16,   "Baby Brigade," Jo Becker and Tejshree Thapa, "Living in Fear Child Soldiers and the Tamil Tigers in Sri Lanka," Human Rights Watch 16, no. 13 (November 2004): 6.

p. 16,   "At first I was . . ." Human Rights Watch. *"Maybe We Live and Maybe We Die. Recruitment and Use of Children by Armed Groups in Syria,"* New York: Human Rights Watch, June 23, 2014, http://www.hrw.org/node/126059/section/2.

p. 17,   "I heard that the rebels . . ." Paul Salopek, "The Guns of Africa," *Seattle Times*, February 27, 2002, Quoted in P. W. Singer. *Children at War.* (New York: Pantheon Books, 2005), 63.

p. 17,   "I returned to my . . ." Finlay Young, "Lost Boys: What Became of Liberia's Child Soldiers?," *Independent* (UK), April 14, 2012, http://www.independent.co.uk/news/world/africa/lost-boys-what-became-of-liberias-child-soldiers-7637101.html.

p. 18,   "Pappy," P. W. Singer, *Children at War* (New York: Pantheon Books, 2005), 72.

p. 18,   "It's like I have . . ." Yvonne E. Keairns, *The Voices of Girl Child Soldiers Philippines*(New York: Quaker United Nations Office, 2003), 19, http://www.quno.org/sites/default/files/resources/The%20voices%20of%20girl%20child%20soldiers_PHILIPPINES.pdf.

p. 18,   "I'm not afraid to die…" Jimmie Briggs, *Innocents Lost: When Child Soldiers Go to War* (New York: Basic Books, 2005), 78.

CHAPTER 3: THE DEN OF DEATH

p. 22,   "When he said . . ." Faith J. H. McDonnell and Grace Akallo, *Girl Soldier: A Story of Hope for Northern Uganda's Children* (Grand Rapids, Michigan: Chosen Books), 2007, 51.

p. 23,   "I was determined . . ." Grace Akallo, "29 April 2009-Grace Akallo at the Security Council," transcript of statement by Grace Akallo to the UN Security Council, http://childrenandarmedconflict.un.org/statement/29-apr-2009-grace-akallo-at-the-security-council.

p. 24,   "The rebels are here," Jesper Strudsholm, "Abducted in the Name of the Lord," *Independent* (UK), June 7, 1998, http://www.independent.co.uk/news/abducted-in-the-name-of-the-lord-1163464.html.

p. 27,   "Sharp stones . . ." Akallo, "I Survived Hell."

p. 27,   "I must take . . ." Grace Akallo, "Former Kony Child Soldier Tells Her Story," an interview with Robin Young, "Here and Now," WBUR Boston, April 19, 2012, www.hearandnow.wbur.org/2012/04/19/kony-child-soldier.

p. 27,   "I'm not a god . . ." DeNeen L. Brown, "A Child's Hell in the Lord's Resistance Army," *Washington Post*, May 10, 2006.

p. 28,   "If one of you . . ." Young, "Former Kony Child Soldier Tells Her Story."

p. 28,   "The first thing . . ." Brown, "A Child's Hell in the Lord's Resistance Army."

p. 28,   "Hunger will teach . . ." McDonnell and Akallo, *Girl Soldier: A Story of Hope for Northern Uganda's Children*, 109.

SOURCES CONTINUED

p. 28,   "It was survival . . ." Priyanka Pruthi, "Grace Akallo Comes Back From the Last Place on Earth,' UNICEF, July 29, 2103, www.unicef.org/protection/57929_69985.html.

p. 29,   "I tried to stop . . ." Young, "Former Kony Child Soldier Tells Her Story."

p. 31,   "bloodshot . . .grandfather," Akallo, "I Survived Hell."

p. 31,   "I was an innocent . . ." Akallo, "29 April 2009-Grace Akallo at the Security Council."

p. 31,   "What makes a girl . . ." Isabelle de Grave, "Former Girl Soldiers Trade One Nightmare for Another," Inter Press Service (UN), June 14, 2012, www.ipsnews.net/2012/06/former-girl-soldiers-trade-one-nightmare-for-another/.

p. 31,   "At first I was . . ." Priyanka Pruthi, "Grace Akallo Comes Back From the Last Place on Earth," UNICEF, July 29, 2103, www.unicef.org/protection/57929_69985.html.

p. 31,   "a den of death . . ." Grace Akallo, "Grace Akallo. Rehabilitated Girl Child Soldier," interviewed by Virginia Swain, TV 13 WCCA, "Imagine Worcester," http://www.wccatv.com/video/imagine-worcester/imagineworcester8.

p. 31,   "jumping over problems . . ." Peggy Noll, "Akallo Grace Grall: From Child Soldiers to University Student," *ReachOut*, New Wineskins Missionary Network, November 2004.

p. 31,   "When I did pray . . ." Akallo, "I Survived Hell."

CHAPTER 4: "GET UP AND GO"

p. 34,   "Every time I tried to pull the trigger..." McDonnell and Akallo, *Girl Soldier: A Story of Hope for Northern Uganda's Children*.

p. 34,   "Get up and go . . ." Grace Akallo, in discussion with the author, May 2007.

p. 36,   "I used to isolate . . ." Pruthi, "Grace Akallo Comes Back From the Last Place on Earth."

p. 37,   "There, I tried in vain . . ." Akallo, "I Survived Hell."

p. 37,   "My parents told me . . ." Henk Rossouw, "An African Tale: First Hell, Then College," *Chronicle of Higher Education* 49, no. 48 (August 8,2003), http://www.nclive.org/cgi-bin/nclsm?url=%22http://search.ebscohost.com.proxy076.nclive.org/login.aspx?direct=true&db=f6h&AN=10537225&site=eds-live%22.

p. 39,   "I know exactly . . ." Joshua Keating, "Negotiator Betty Bigombe on Kony's 15 Minutes," *Foreign Policy*, March 14, 2012.

p. 39,   "I want Joseph Kony . . ." "Former Kony Child Soldiers Tells Her Story," *Here & Now*, April 19, 2012, http://hereandnow.wbur.org/2012/04/19/kony-child-soldier.

CHAPTER 5: ADVOCATE FOR JUSTICE AND PEACE

p. 45,   "Some of them . . ." Clair MacDougall, "When Liberian Child Soldiers Grow Up," *Newsweek*, July 31, 2013, www.newsweek.com/2013/07/31/when-liberian-child-soldiers-grow-237780.html.

p. 48,   "Children are the seeds . . ." Sara Cameron in cooperation with UNICEF, *Out of War: True Stories from the Front Lines of the Children's Movement for Peace in Colombia.* (New York: Scholastic Press, 2001), 176.

p. 50,   "If you are alive…" Ishmael Beah, *A Long Way Home: Memoirs of a Boy Soldier* (New York: Farrar, Straus and Giroux), 54.

p. 51,   "I loved helping . . ." Akallo, "I Survived Hell."

p. 51,   "If a kid, . . ." Grace Akallo, in discussion with the author, May 2007.

p. 51,   "maybe some day . . ." Pruthi, "Grace Akallo Comes Back From the Last Place on Earth."

p. 51,   "I have told . . ." Akallo, "29 April 2009-Grace Akallo at the Security Council."

p. 53,   "I may never know . . . help them," Akallo, "I Survived Hell."

BIBLIOGRAPHY

Akallo, Grace. In discussion with the author, May 2007.

———."I Survived Hell." As told to Deann Alford. *Ignite Your Faith* 65, no. 8 (March 2007). www.christianitytoday.com/iyf/truelifestories/ithappenedtome/7.38.html.

———. "29 April 2009-Grace Akallo at the Security Council," transcript of statement by Grace Akallo to the UN Security Council. http://childrenandarmedconflict.un.org/statement/29-apr-2009-grace-akallo-at-the-security-council.

———. "Former Kony Child Soldier Tells Her Story." Interviewed by Robin Young, "Here and Now," WBUR Boston, April 19, 2012. www.hearandnow.wbur.org/2012/04/19/kony-child-soldier.

———. "Grace Akallo. Rehabilitated Girl Child Soldier." Interviewed by Virginia Swain, TV 13 WCCA, "Imagine Worcester." April 9, 2009. http://www.wccatv.com/video/imagine-worcester/imagineworcester8.

Beah, Ishmael. *A Long Way Gone: Memoirs of a Boy Soldier.* New York: Farrar, Straus and Giroux, 2007.

Briggs, Jimmie. *Innocents Lost: When Child Soldiers Go to War.* New York: Basic Books, 2005.

Brown, Deen L. "A Child's Hell in the Lord's Resistance Army." *Washington Post*, May 10, 2006.

Cameron, Sara. *Out of War: True Stories from the Front Lines of the Children's Movement for Peace in Colombia.* New York: Scholastic Press, 2001.

Child Soldiers. Global Report 2008. London: Coalition to Stop the Use of Child Soldiers, 2008.

Chrobog, Karim, director. *Emmanuel Jal: War Child.* A documentary.

Dallaire, Roméo. *They Fight Like Soldiers, They Die Like Children.* New York: Walker & company, 2011.

Deng, Alephonsion, Benson Deng and Benjamin Ajak, with Judy A. Bernstein. *They Poured Fire on Us from the Sky: The True Story of Three Lost Boys From Sudan.* New York: Public Affairs, 2005.

de Grave, Isabelle. "Former Girl Soldiers Trade One Nightmare for Another." Inter Press Service (UN), June 14, 2012.www.ipsnews.net/2012/06/former-girl-soldiers-trade-one-nightmare-for-another/.

Education For All Global Monitoring Team: *The Hidden Crisis: Armed Conflict and Education.* Paris: UNESCO, 2011.

Eichstaedt, Peter. *First Kill Your Family: Child Soldiers of Uganda and the Lord's Resistance Army.* Chicago. Illinois: Lawrence Hill Books, 2009.

Hermes, Will. "Straight Out of Sudan: A Child Soldier Raps." *New York Times*, October 2, 2005.

Human Rights Watch. *Children in the Ranks: The Maoists' Use of Child Soldiers in Nepal.* New York: Human Rights Watch. February 2, 2007. http://www.hrw.org/reports/2007/02/01/children-ranks-0.

———. The Christmas Massacres. LRA Attacks on Civilians in Northern Congo. New York: Human Rights Watch. February 16, 2009. http://www.hrw.org/reports/2009/02/16/christmas-massacres-0.

———. "Maybe We Live and Maybe We Die. Recruitment and Use of Children by Armed Groups in Syria." New York: Human Rights Watch. June 23, 2014. http://www.hrw.org/node/126059/.

———. *Trail of Death. LRA Atrocities in Northeastern Congo.* New York: Human Rights Watch, 2010.http://www.hrw.org/reports/2010/03/28/trail-death.

———. *You'll Learn Not to Cry: Child Combatants in Colombia.* New York: Human Rights Watch, 2003. http://www.hrw.org/reports/2003/colombia0903/colombia0903.pdf.

IRIN (UN Office for the Coordination of Humanitarian Affairs). July 3, 2014. http://www.irinnews.org/report/100300/analysis-targeted-assistance-needed-for-drc-s-former-child-soldiers.

Iweala, Uzodinma. *Beasts of No Nation: A Novel.* New York: HarperCollins, 2005.

Kahn, Leora, ed. *Child Soldiers.* Brooklyn, New York: Powerhouse Books, 2008.

Keairns, Yvonne E. *The Voices of Girl Child Soldiers Philippines.* New York: Quaker United Nations Office, 2003. http://www.quno.org/sites/default/files/resources/The%20voices%20of%20girl%20child%20soldiers_PHILIPPINES.pdf.

Keating, Joshua. "Negotiator Betty Bigombe on Kony's 15 Minutes." *Foreign Policy*, March 14, 2012.

Lineberry, Cate. "The Boys of War." *New York Times*, October 4, 2011.

MacDougall, Clair. "When Liberian Child Soldiers Grow Up." *Newsweek*, July 31, 2013. www.newsweek.com/2013/07/31/when-liberian-child-soldiers-grow-237780.html.

BIBLIOGRAPHY CONTINUED

McDonnell, Faith J. H., and Grace Akallo. *Girl Soldier: A Story of Hope for Northern Uganda's Children*. Grand Rapids, Michigan: Chosen Books, 2007.

Mydans, Seth. "For Child Leaders of Burmese Rebels a Strange and Lonely Jungle Life." *New York Times*, July 20, 2000.

Noll, Peggy. "Akallo Grace Grall: From Child Soldiers to University Student." *ReachOut*. New Wineskins Missionary Network, November 2004.

Ojewska, Natalia. "Analysis: Targeted assistance needed for DRC's former child soldiers."

Piasecki, Jerry. *Marie: In the Shadow of the Lion. A Humanitarian Novel*. New York: United Nations, 2001.

Pruthi, Priyanka. "Grace Akallo Comes Back From the Last Place on Earth." UNICEF, July 29, 2103. www.unicef.org/protection/57929_69985.html.

Rossouw, Henk. "An African Tale: First Hell, Then College." *Chronicle of Higher Education* 49, no. 48 (August 8,2003). http://www.nclive.org/cgi-bin/nclsm?url=%22http://search. ebscohost.com.proxy076.nclive.org/login.aspx?direct=true&db=f6h&AN=10537225&site=e ds-live%22.

Sawyer, Kem Knapp, and Jon Sawyer. *Congo's Children*. Washington, DC: Pulitzer Center on Crisis Reporting, 2014.

Scroggins, Deborah. *Emma's War: An Aid Worker, a Warlord, Radical Islam, and the Politics of Oil—A True Story of Love and Death in Sudan*. New York: Pantheon Books, 2002.

Singer, P. W. *Children at War*. New York: Pantheon Books, 2005.

Strudsholm, Jesper. "Abducted in the Name of the Lord." *Independent* (UK), June 7, 1998. http://www.independent.co.uk/news/abducted-in-the-name-of-the-lord-1163464.html.

Temmerman, Els De. *Aboke Girls: Children Abducted in Northern Uganda*. Kampala, Uganda: Fountain Publisher, 2001.

"The Twin Terrors." *Time*. February 7, 2000. http://content.time.com/time/world/ article/0,8599,2054474,00.html

UNICEF. *State of the World's Children 2014*. New York: United Nations, 2014.

Young, Finlay. "Lost Boys: What Became of Liberia's Child Soldiers?" *Independent* (UK), April 14, 2012. http://www.independent.co.uk/news/world/africa/lost-boys-what-became-of-liberias-child-soldiers-7637101.html.

WEB SITES

CHILD SOLDIERS INTERNATIONAL: Disseminates research on child soldiers and advocates for the protection of children's rights (formerly the Coalition to Stop the Use of Child Soldiers).
http://www.child-soldiers.org/

EVERYDAY GANDHIS: Promotes peace-building and aids former child soldiers in Liberia.
http://www.everydaygandhis.org/

INVISIBLE CHILDREN: Brings awareness to abuses by the Lord's Resistance Army and advocates for an end to the use of child soldiers.
http://invisiblechildren.com/

ROMÉO DALLAIRE CHILD SOLDIER INITIATIVE: Supports training, research and advocacy. Founded by Canadian humanitarian and former Force Commander for the UN Assistance Mission for Rwanda Roméo Dallaire.
http://www.childsoldiers.org/

THE RESOLVE LRA CRISIS INITIATIVE: Supports research, reporting and advocacy to end the violence perpetrated by the Lord's Resistance Army
http://www.theresolve.org/

UNITED AFRICANS FOR WOMEN AND CHILDREN RIGHTS: Advocates for policy change to promote economic development and end violence against women and girls. Founded by Grace Akallo.
http://www.africanwomenrights.org/

UNITED NATIONS OFFICE OF THE SPECIAL REPRESENTATIVE OF THE SECRETARY-GENERAL FOR CHILDREN IN ARMED CONFLICT: Works to end child recruitment and sexual violence. Supports the "Children, Not Soldiers" campaign.
http://childrenandarmedconflict.un.org/

INDEX

PHOTO CREDITS

Cover: Andrea Bruce / The Washington Post via Getty Images

1: Courtesy of UNICEF

2: MICHAEL KAMBER / KRT / Newscom

3: Chris Hondros / Getty Images

5: Luiz Rampelotto / ZUMAPRESS / Newscom

6-7: Sudarsan Raghavan / TNS / ZUMAPRESS

10-11: Courtesy U.S.National Archives

13: Courtesy of Library of Congress

14: Hulton Archive / Getty Images

16: Ezz Zanoun / ZUMA Press / Newscom

18-19: Thierry Falise / LightRocket via Getty Images

20-21: Associated Press

24: Associated Press

27: Courtesy of the Internet Archive

32-33: STEPHEN MORRISON / EPA / Newscom

34-35: Micah Albert / ZUMA

38-39: Associated Press

40-41: Tom Williams / Roll Call Photos / Newscom

43: NIC BOTHMA / EPA / Newscom

45: Liba Taylor / Alamy

47: JEAN-MARC FERRE/REUTERS / Newscom

49: Bea Ahbeck / Fremont Argus / ZUMAPRESS / Newscom

50: Courtesy of UNICEF

52-53: WENN Ltd / Alamy